Greetings from My Girlie Leisure Place

Greetings from My Girlie Leisure Place

Sharon Mesmer

Greetings from My Girlie Leisure Place
© 2015 Sharon Mesmer
19 18 17 16 15   1 2 3 4 5

Design & composition: Shanna Compton, shannacompton.com
Cover images: "The Little Pets," artist unknown. Vintage trade card for Scott's Emulsion (Scott & Bowne, New York & London), 1887. "Reine Marguerite Pyramidale Pivoine Variee," artist unknown. French seed packet, 1920s. Public domain images sourced from olddesignshop.com.

Published by Bloof Books
www.bloofbooks.com
New Jersey

Bloof Books are printed in the USA by Spencer Printing. Booksellers, libraries, and other institutions may order direct from us by contacting sales@bloofbooks.com. POD copies are distributed via Ingram, Baker & Taylor, and other wholesalers. Individuals may purchase our books direct from our website, from online retailers such as Amazon.com, or request them from their favorite bookstores.

Please support your local independent bookseller whenever possible.

ISBN-13: 978-0-9965868-1-8
ISBN-10: 0-9965868-1-4
1. American poetry—21st century. 2. Poets, American—21st century.

♾ This paper meets the requirements of ANSI/NISO Z39.48-1992 (Permanence of Paper).

For David

CONTENTS

Assemblage, Moeity, Propinquity

Three: Someday We Shall All Say Yes to Death

Hello, Everyone

Hello, Everyone

Hello, everyone.
I am a new writer
and I am currently working on
a fictional novel
that is also fantasy.
I have not read much fantasy
except for *The Chronicles of Narnia*,
but I think the best thing
is just use imagination.
My favorite quote is
"You are only limited
by your imagination
and the laws in your area."

I have a fantasy book idea.
Here is a little bit of it.
It takes place in a world
where kings, knights, wizards,
princesses, pirates, mermaids,
elves and hobbits are.
I might also include
giants, dwarves, dragons,
centaurs, fauns, unicorns,
gods and goddesses,
bigfoot zombies
and wookiees.
But I think that if I want to have
mythical creatures
I should read up on them
because I know very little
about the subject.

I have another problem.
I have drawn a map
of the mythical world
and I like how it looks,
but I don't know if I can
draw it again in a bigger size.
I guess I would have to get
one of my friends that can draw
to draw it.

I'm a dreamer.
I'm also a workaholic hippie.
I think I'm turning into a pirate
or maybe a gypsy punk.
I've heard pirates
were the original punks.
But what about zombies?
They were probably
around before pirates
because there've always been the dead,
and if you have the dead
you also have to have the undead.
And now that we're in the future
we can have zombie pirate robots,
or even ninja zombie pirate robots.
I'd like to see
a ninja zombie pirate robot wizard
that is made of some kind of meat.
Preferably bacon.
It could come with the book,
freeze-dried of course
in a little package.
But if that's too difficult,
maybe just a tiny freeze-dried
bacon unicorn bookmark.

I wonder if in medieval times
people ate unicorn bacon
and if it tasted like
our modern bacon
of today.
I know I'm just a 33-year-old nerd
in Lewisburg Ohio
with ever-shifting Brangelina crisis alerts
but I think my fictional fantasy novel
could be good.
I also think I could perform
on *New Year's Rockin' Eve*
with some horsey-chested man
like Robert Plant in his prime.
We could be the Captain and Tennille
of a medieval fantasy world,
and I'd wear one of those tall pointy hats
with the long scarf attached
and the Captain/Robert Plant and I would sing
"Havin' My Baby,"
and then the baby would appear
and it would be a gnome.
Or dwarf.
Whatever.
It wouldn't matter
that we're both men
because of how advanced
today's society is becoming.
But I think Robert Plant might care
because I know he likes girls.
I don't know
about the Captain, though.

ONE

I Am a Lonely Oneironaut

I Want to Expose Myself for Love of the People

I want to expose myself for love of the people.
I want to expose myself, and smile, and cogitate quietly, for love of the people.
Extraordinary goals require extraordinary action, and so
I want to expose myself in the grocery store,
eating deli meats and cookies right off the shelves,
for love of the people.
I don't want more opium than Thailand.
I just love myself, and the people, so much that I want to be a better person,
and take pride in the things I can do, because I love me, and so I seek
to expose myself for love of the people, and of me.
I just flew in from Vegas, where I exposed myself for love of the people.
I wanted the people of Vegas to laugh, to cry, to hate, to love, to feel that life
is about reading and sharing and gambling
and exposing.
And so I was exposing myself to girls who are in need and vulnerable.
When a developing girl asked me, "Do you want to have the opportunity
to expose yourself to some laundry?" I had to answer:
"Anything goes."
Because I don't want to achieve immortality through my signature
coffee-colored popovers.
I want to achieve immortality through exposing myself.
Invite me over, and one thing will lead to another, and then in the morning,
if you die a painful death and I bury your body in the backyard,
and it's similar to the way Europeans love to smoke, and I love smoking,
and you love traveling, then I will expose myself to a bus full of people
stranded in traffic.
I want to become a beacon for Maintaining Your Dignity
While Exposing Yourself for Love of the People.
I am not sure who my biological parents are, but I believe their goal was
to become Pokémon masters, and continue to get with baby squirrels.
If Jesus has a pet baby squirrel, and it jumps on me, could I still expose myself
for love of the people?

I want Mexican nuns to be victims of my love.
Also Oreos, Dr. Pepper and Cheetos.
And Mother Teresa.
Actually, I want to be Mother Teresa, victim of love, getting exposed to
and exposing for, the love of the people.
If my poetry aims to achieve anything, it's to deliver people from the limited ways
they expose themselves in grocery stores, in Vegas, Thailand or Neverland
for love of the people.
I will write a poem later, but right now I am enjoying exposing myself
as an intelligent, sensitive human, with the soul of a clown, and not just any clown,
but a clown deer, who committed suicide after being banished from the forest
after he was caught by other deer exposing himself
during a fawn birthday party
on the White House lawn
for love of the people.
And deer.

I Am Now Bringing Everything to the Path

Working class, ethnic, unemployable and obscure,
I *am* the Polish church in anguish.
And that's why I am now bringing everything to the Path.
Granted, my "girlie leisure place" YouTube video
is ludicrous, but no matter where you are, chances are
you can crack a window and hear a cow moo,
a cow who is bringing everything to the Path, too.
I am bringing my see-through green glass typewriter
with its famous trademark of illegal firearms
in curlicue *sgraffito*, Italian-style, on the space bar
to the Path, plus eating my seed concoctions with a spoon
(and secretly looking for a Path with fruit).
Some semioticians say that all the Elvis sightings suggest
the atavistic power of the Dionysus myth
in the human psyche,
but I say that's just Elvis bringing improved spatial orientation
to the Path, as he dances flat-footed with arms raised
and palms held flat
in a sea-green merkin,
and curled Grecian wig complete with a wreath
of gleaming copper grapes.
"The Path," he says, "is not manufactured; the Path just is—
thus, too, my art."
Thus too my own personal Path,
to which I am now bringing
extraordinary contortions, including a sort of
sideways hopscotch
interrupted by a few seconds of statuesque immobility,
on one foot,
as I descend from a nest of shit flies who are reproducing
in a festooned silver circle.
But where is Jesus Christ in all this?

Uh, did you know I'm bringing Jesus to the Path, too?
Because I once had a professor who said it was high time
to bring everything together into one killer Jesus—
on the other hand,
your Jesus friends who want to bring actual killers to the Path
should probably just stay home.
You say Hollywood whispered your name and said
"Why don't you bring your big ass on over to the Path?"
I say you are living on one of the moons of Harry Connick, Jr.
But that's okay,
'cause once you start bringin' that big ass on over to the Path,
the Path itself is gonna be bringin' it.

I Am Cocked Up from Overpower

The God of the overpowering I AM
is in ME now that I am
cocked up from overpower.

And it is the I AM of lost promos
and hologram hero cards
that I now am

a cocked-up washerwoman of labial wings
except I wish I weren't so familiar
with the whole cocked-up aporia

of my overpower.
The odd thing is
that I am getting kind of dusty

from cock-licking the moors.
Each sentience of overpower seems
a cocked-up overpowering of ambiance

over power lines
finessing it
into battle stance.

I am an amateur radio rooster
for cocked-up overpower
using a vampire mayo that is

light in flavor
to eliminate the perplexed logic of all Belizean
warlock action plans.

A rockin' cock-maid splays
in a room, in a fiery rain
and burns all enemies
with the CWAZIEST agility aspects of cock.
She is there because you wish to learn about,
or have already chosen,

the dark path of prairie venom
which her cocked-up overpower reveals to be
Amazon cocking up Kindle's
bodybuilding nursery school in Canada.

If you love your hog of oneself
grinding up against a dirty guitar
kung fu-style

in negative space
then you are cocked up with lollipops,
doggie style.

Expect toy anal ATMs next.

I Am a Lonely Oneironaut, in Need of Salutary Grounding

I am a lonely ragtag mushroom cowboy
lonesome as the winter ocean
waking from a battlestar
walking lost and lonely
galaxy-tipping lonely
lonely and in love with
this poor city and the whole world
singing "lonely boy lonely girl
suddenly soul searching"
Miss Demure
lucidly dreaming
lonely drifter Karen—
lonely schnozz, longest walk—
lord of the living room lonely
professional adult orphan
neglectful of volition
taking crap on two continents
and always getting rained on
by amateur clouds
lonely

Oh, solitary psychedelic alchemist
Oh, twisted oneironaut:
tell me GPS gets lonely
tell me déjà vu is lonely
tell me the antipodean dream
at the end of time
is lonely

tell me

I Blame the Black Man for My Goat Paths

I blame the black man for my goat paths.
I blame my father, who was a goat herder.
I blame Adam Ant's "ethnic confusion."
I blame the yellow man, too, and Daniel Boone.

I blame middle-aged Koreans with legs and lungs like mountain goats,
and the new snowmobile helmet head protection.
I blame all the cock I've ever had in my mouth for my not being vegan,
and—look, Dad: *baby* goat paths!

I blame *Days of our Lives* because this one character totally got fired
and they put another guy in his place, and I can't even watch him because,
you know, he's not the same guy, and what am I going to watch now,
one of those judge shows? I'm studying to be a second wife.

I blame the badass Red Lobster feast I am still trying to shake off.
I blame the fat American Enterprise Institute poster hobo who fucked my
co-worker, and then told her that mongoose po-po guarantees a do-over.
I blame motherfucking mongoose po-po for foiling my terrorist plots.

I blame gay adult coloring books where Disney hard-sells its cheap ovarian bling,
the black man, all current and former chancellors of the University of Illinois,
clown vagina, clown porn gags, git invalids, the unknown Berenstain Bear (Nacho),
and the fact that ducks waddle.

I blame compassionate conservatives for the rumor that I started a show
called *Movebusters*, in which I bust moves on the current scourge of white hipsters
incorporating the Swedish vowel *å*, pronounced as the English *au* as in the word *vault*,
because the Swedish vowel *å* is closer in pronunciation to the long vowel *ā*

in English, as in the word *blame*: a mushy, extruded diphthong
for which I blame Speaker of the House John Boehner's hovering, disembodied

Cap'n Crunch eyebrows over Octomom as she navigates a post-Jewish Dr. Seuss—
who was in fact a stoic Lutheran ably navigating all the Cat in the Hat's goat paths—
through the weary world of dick.

But mostly I blame the black man.

I Think I Might Be Facebook-Pregnant

I'm against glamorizing teen pregnancy!
Yes I'm a teenager. No I am not pregnant,
high, or about to steal mommyhood rights from Facebook.
To Those Who Are 6–8 Weeks Pregnant, I Salute You!

I'm worried about telling people I'm pregnant
'cause then they will LOL about how I was a fat cow
before and now I'm fatter and plus full of apps.
How to avoid "mailbox miscarriage"?

Does Facebook hate the pregnant female form?
I think people are terrified and have gone beyond
loving the stork's stressed messenger for bringing
slutty teenage girls and stupid guys together.

I got pregnant when I followed a unicorn into a temple.
Now I'm three months pregnant with a dim-witted unicorn baby,
and am wondering when it might be appropriate to
"doom the wolf"?

What is a "uterus," Mr. Pregnant?
My gorgeous tiny uni-cow is sex-wishing a genie unicorn
to get itself pregnant now.
Pregnant uni-cow-wife baby shock!

I Think I Might Be Having Seizures

Uh-oh: I think I might be having seizures.
Absence seizures, atonic seizures,
maybe even benign rolandic epilepsy.

Then there's childhood absence,
cyclonic presence,
frontal lobe and febrile denseness.
Infantile spasms with jaundice,
juvenile myoclonic tension,
Hot-Water-and-Kleenex syndrome.

Also Landau-Kleffner psychosis,
mitochondrial disorder,
progressive chthonic reflex epilepsy
mixed with bilateral catamenia.
I think I have that.

Rasmussen's syndrome,
simple secondarily generalized temporal lobe fits,
tonic-clonic chthonic reflex,
Psychomotor Limbic Dysfunction,
and definitely status epilepticus.

And here comes the abdominal akinetic autonomic seizure,
Massive Bilateral Drop in Consciousness,
and focal Jacksonian gelastic seizure
brought on by one nocturnal multifocal motor-Lafora
pseudoseizure, because it's been snaining
(snowing + raining)
all fucking day.

And lest we forget: sensory seizures,
subtle seizures,
and sylvan visual reflex withdrawal seizures.

Amongst others.

I Am Mormon Hot

I am hot.
Mormon hot.
Oh my effing God, I am sick hot.
Ick hot.
Ich-bin-ein-Mormon hot.
Mormon-fight-in-a-clown-car hot.
And that includes soup.
World's-oldest-freestanding-pagoda-visited-by-Mormons hot.
Married-Mormon-graduate-students-involved-in-poon-pregret hot.
Tragicomic-Mormon-homosexual-at-war-in-California-face-down-in-the-stun-bath-
weeping-hot-tears-behind-3D-glasses hot.

Feminist Mormon Housewives + Bath Time = hot.
Mormon Mommy Wars >>> The Agony That Is Weaning:
        hot showers, self-pump, bacon and hot dogs . . .
Hot.
Postum . . . Twinkies . . . hormones . . . *The Book of Mormon* tells us
that unattractive women are really hot Mormon men who,
once inside the body of Mom, mimic estrogen.
Even though the Mormon church is based on
a 14-year-old's dreams and fantasies,
the Mormon mega-dance phenomenon—
fog machines, cool deejay, earsplitting music, wallflowers, cliques—
is not just cute but four full hours of profuse palpating man sweat.
Palpating Mormon man sweat.
Hot . . .

I'm blaming Mormon hormone replacement therapy
that Women are from Venus, Men are from where God
has blonde chicks hanging all over him.
Celebrated Christmas greeting amanuensis Laura Bush
must be a Mormon,

'cause if you've ever looked into her eyes,
you know she'd be the first to share a comforting bowl
of hot, buttered polygamist squirrel
with the entire hormone-charged mosh pit of 2008's Mormon Prom.
Which is where, by the way, I found my very own
Mormon-hot utopian dream:
twelve handsome returned missionaries
eating deep-fried corn snacks made from an extrusion of talk show hosts and athletes
in a hot tub UFO time machine.

Hot!

I Have Always Wanted an Emu

It takes guts to goose Johnny Carson
with an emu.
That's why I've always wanted
an emu.

My emu will have more plastic surgery
than Cher, Demi Moore,
and the entire waitstaffs of all the Hooters,
combined.

I just discovered the whole emu scene
twelve days ago.
Now I want to purchase
an elegant Elizabethan mansion
and live there with my emu.
Their sound is incredibly deep,
like European dudes.

The main reason I love emus
is that people suck.
It is impossible
for emus to suck.
They don't have lips.

I also love emus because
no one in my family can fly
but we all run really fast.
We have three toes on each foot.
I'm very curious too.
I stick my nose into everything
and if I don't understand something
I stomp on it.

I love Triscuits too.
I believe them to be
the best crackers ever
in the whole history
of crackers.
I also love the new and improved
Stardust Ballroom.
I have received double
in payback blessings
for every rotten thing that happened
to me and my emu
the last time we went
ballroom dancing there—
someone removed my pants
and slathered me with
orange marmalade.
The police
were NOT amused.

Here is the first poem
I ever wrote
about emus:

I love emus
whose color is black.
My father took my Legos
and won't give them back.

Don't tell anyone,
but I also love
sexy emu amputees.
I heard emus are prudes
but I also heard
Posh Spice sleeps alone.

It's insane how she resembles
a raptor.

If you're coulrophobic
(fear of clowns),
don't be afraid.
You can't love a clown
or an emu
if you don't
love yourself first.

I Am Disappointed

I am disappointed
that my vision of a vibrant rabbit community was dispelled.

I am disappointed
that it's not OK to pee on the tire
'cause then the business would go in the fields.

If a man can pee into a woman's vagina, can she pee for both of them?
If not, I am disappointed.

I know I have bad luck.
So to make up I just hold my breath as long as I can so that my body
can use as much of the nutrients as possible.
That way, I am never disappointed.

Air seems so ordinary.
But where would we be without our friends
the even-toed ungulates?

Nativity chimeras?
Disappointing.

I am now speaking out against gargoyles.
I have worn a fly mask and baby blanket without issues,
so what are these fly mask-wearing gargoyles doing?
Should I just go up to these pony-club types and squeeze?

Surrounded and traversed by Goat Expeditionary Squadrons,
I am disappointed in "NORAD Tracks Santa."
Let's not abilify that mofo.

I am really very disappointed in Dean Koontz
for publishing a Bible study that was supposed to help with weight loss.
I won't go into detail, but I am disappointed . . .

And how about the emotionally stunted adult
(i.e., Weird Library Guy)
liking girls and throwing all kinds of shade?
That just reinforces condescension.

And what about your standard 80s-porn-chic short shorts and tube socks
evoking Beyoncé's self-righteous birthday concert?
Don't.

I personally find it disappointing
that an NFL player with an enlarged heart
can blindly drift into market-driven metrosexuality.
Queer male identity is certainly due for an overhaul.

I am disappointed
that I teleported into Montana with an army
and yet no one attacked me . . .

I am disappointed that John McCain had to withdraw from Ann Coulter.
What is this shit that I paid to see?

The Junior Mint Introduction to Basketball
being limited to only 20 kindergartens
should have warranted at least 100 more robocalls expressing concerns.

Eat soap because your mom says you look like Dopey from *Snow White*?
I'll rip your head off and shit down your neck!

Wake up feeling like P. Diddy?
Suck my dick, whitey.

Cake is a lie?
Watch me bust a cap in your ass.

Pig innards and dog poo on the ceiling?
Right. After time, they'll become your friends.

I Am Against Panda Bears Making Out

I have not been making blanket accusations against corporations,
only against panda bears making out.
I love animals, and have been to see panda bears in four cities.
Despite all this, I am against panda bears making out.

Surgeons may eat their own, but I fell out of my chair at this one:
PANDA BEAR MAKING OUT, M.D.

I am not against making money,
and I certainly realize that competition is ultimately good
for the panda bear who likes to make out.
But what I am against is the continued use of
"Who Let the Dogs Out?" for solemn occasions.
I'd prefer Sade's Super Bowl version of
"Who Let the Panda Bears Making Out Out?"

My gut feeling has always been that I am against
plotting an approach to the young panda bear making out.
But how should I broach the topic with the young panda bear
who is, at this moment, making out?

Why did I give a panda bear a DVD about 9/11?
Because there is a principle
which is the proof
that while I'm not a believer,
I'm not a denier either,
of the rights of panda bears to make out.

Like Smokey the Bear before him,
a panda bear making out swirls down the road
so silently that we can barely make out
all the magical sounds of him making out.

Okay: panda bears who make out,
please come to my house in Hawaii.
I'll have plenty of panda bear cookies.
And we'll make out.

I Discovered Pain

I discovered pain.
But that was after I discovered
Chuck Norris's real name (Carlos)
and the cramp-giving power of his mullet
when pitted against a bog oak.

I discovered pain,
but that was after I discovered
the secret parody set of Nobel Peace Prizes
disguised as the mountain men who lick hallucinating Irishmen
in an enchanted forest.

I discovered pain when I discovered
Paul McCartney advancing his aims with Mr. Pillow-Smotherer-Dude
in a struggle under a gangway window
as voices rose in protest, and wild horses shambled
in the half-light of a same-same Milky Way.
Three stalwart robins approached,
intimidating me.

And that's probably when I discovered
that Freemason needle freaks actually discovered pain
in the magnetic flux lines that do not move
despite the Lorentz force acting on them inside a current-carrying
Type-II superconductor, rocketing through a wormhole.
And that no one really gives a shit about
nacreous baboon openings,
or mullet challenges to boil colonization
on the edible cockles of a penis.

I discovered pain
in a moment of repose,
in a proud ravaged harbor enclosed
in a bog oak.

I Know Well the #1 Thing Keeping Me from Really Learning How to Knit Is My Own Deep Inner Shrug

This is the first ballerina shrug that I've made.
I've gifted it to my Deep Inner Monologue.
Here I am, outside in the ten-degree night, but I'm not cold—
I have my boyfriend Obama's love to keep me warm.
Plus the shrug. Tonight, more knitting on my lace U-neck dovetail
multiseason vest/shawl.

In between screwing and complaining about screwing,
I decided to stop all the Deep Inner Turmoil by frogging over the black abyss
of a moat surrounding my Deep Lady Cocoon by fashioning
an open-work diamond-design Obama shrug for my kitty.
Why should Obama tea cozies have all the fun?

Yep, Obama is my boyfriend, even though we are usually separated
by about 20,000 people. Yup, me and Obama are officially an item.
What we have is special. I'm waiting with bated breath to hear
what Jenn and Erika have to say about it, once I tell them.

You know my first name (Archturiat) has some deep spiritual meaning.
It means "my ADD may largely be the result of wading through the deep waters
of an Olympic pullover with knitting needles lodged in my ear, ooooh . . .
wind chimes." I guess my deep dark secret is . . .
I love Monday mornings.
They are a good match for Obama's skin tone.

No court of law could keep me from warming myself with my own
Obama open crewel-work knitted blanky wrapped over my shoulders.
I read my book and drift contentedly to sleep.
But then I awake suddenly from a loud crash heard deep within my
very first from-scratch garment—a webcam of 100% virgin merino from Korea,
in deep chocolate and grayish beige, no grief,
with an inner core of regular wool.

I scream "Obama!" and he rescues me.
We find God and run self-help workshops for inner-city children.

A night at the seaside with my boyfriend Obama reveals to me the splendors of
Deep Calm Knitting. He sits there staring with his mouth agape.
But I just keep knitting, and providing food for our wee baby.
Why freak out?
Just because my plum trees are actually cherry?

I Lost My Beatnik Antlers on the Grassy Knoll—Help Me, JFK

I lost my khakis and my hair smoosh
and my craft beer/Telly Savalas shrine.
I lost my *History of Maple Urine Disease* on the grassy knoll,
and my trainable kielbasa.

I lost my eatable narc pants.
I was told I had lost my reason.
I lost my A-Rod beanstalk mojo on the grassy knoll
but I found my Christmas spliff.

Scully, Mulder, I will be a doctor,
but I need my Ryan Seacrest Is a Kitty blanket first.
Cuba has Santería, Haiti has Voodoo, and I have my
Abraham Lincoln's Birthday Does Irish Cheerleaders at Madison Square Garden pass
       . . . oops: had.

Jean Valjean's balls are on the rebound from Napoleon,
but don't look for them on the grassy knoll.
Also lost are Broadway memories of Sylvia Plath
and Rachael Ray's My Little e-Pony giveaway.

I hear Maytag refrigerators are polling the Elephant Man's spider bite
about Tom of Finland's minimum wage petition.
Apparently it's also gone missing on the grassy knoll.
Now I don't feel so alone.

Russell Crowe's Peanut Corporation is also lost,
as well as Canadian television's *Why Do I Have Green Poop?* NASCAR series.
Too bad about Neil Patrick Harris's Spanglish movie *Wampum the Sky Warrior*
(and *Wampum Reloaded: Zombie Apocalypse Credit Union*).

Whatever happened to Marie Osmond's Deluxe Dead Baby Pills Patch™?
And *Freak-Out on Lesbian Mountain* starring groundhog puppets and sponsored by Abilify?
And where are Hosni Mubarak's pics of America's most voluptuous MILF members
of the Loyal Order of Benevolent Toilet Dogs?
I think we know the answer.

My live sponge birth control Pay-per-view?
My Prednisone-induced diarrhea tracking number?
My cat's resignation letter to Maya Angelou's Power Rangers' *Diaper-Lover Stories Night*?

Help me, JFK!

This Poet

This Poet

What visible corporeal form does this poet present?
In what traditional nuances does she come "dressed"?
Does she suggest a hidden half-life of carefully maintained traditions?
Or does she eschew these nuances,
in favor of breaking off relations with the past?
If so, do earlier assertions lose their verity?
If not, is there a fraught relationship with the past?

Does this poet successfully express "commence"?
Does she stand up without weakness to say her piece,
ignoring criticisms or challenges to her origin story?
Does she demonstrate the ability to successfully streamline
the long history of prosody into the treasured figure
of a golden human woman with kitten hands?

How does this poet reveal her basic nature,
her mortal wound?
Is it through her choice of dog?
And does that choice reveal (perhaps unwittingly) that, at nightfall,
her mind is too often beset with danger and blame,
and wondering about that wavering light behind the viaduct?
Does the inclusion of a viaduct support an as yet undeveloped
theory of beauty?
If so, what is her relation, if any, to beauty?
From what mud has this poet arisen, or
from what known or as yet undiscovered star has she descended?
How does she "sprout"?
How does her dog "sprout"?
Does her dog "sprout"?

Are there inevitable entanglements with syntactical intention
that this poet successfully manages to avoid?

If not, what are the unfortunate consequences?
Is she so deeply in disagreement with her own sentience
that she fails to teach social skills, the patience for opportunity,
the ability to recognize and negotiate subtle gateways?
How does she compromise/express uniformity, or at least meet halfway
the need for the establishment of such gateways?
Does she successfully compete in free-market fashion
while keeping the engine of her competition hidden?

What is her relation, if any, to beauty?
Does she seem to suggest the quantifying of such an unstable,
unreliable (and even vilifying) property as beauty?

First of all, does she even suggest an instability?
Does she lay personal claim to unquantifiability?
Are any properties at all suggested?
Or does she automatically devolve to mirroring?
If so, is there a hidden meaning in the mirroring,
and by what methods (grounded in the text or otherwise located)
can it be accurately gleaned?

Does she suggest the presence of a body crown?
And then provide specific guidances about how to ground,
frame, and then leverage that body crown for greater gains?
Can she adequately assess, then communicate—
in normative syntax, with a clear purview—
the purpose and worth of her own (markedly obvious) body crown?
And can she successfully balance that crown against the pure gold
of tradition, spun from air?

Does she make small gains that can be noticed, tracked?
And is this because of some carefully preserved piquant fragment
of a fraught past?
Does this fragment allow her to provide, without fanfare, and little preparation,
her own humble supper?

Does it confer the ability to traverse a thorny path carefully, gracefully, successfully,
and, while navigating, maintain balance and harmony
in the midst of sudden, irreversible—even tragic—
changes to the landscape?

Can this poet's many obstacles,
so obviously and firmly set, and working against one another,
maintain a unified field, or at least work to neutralize unexpected attacks
from hostile, outside sources, on the poet's core beliefs?
Can these obstacles, through their own natures and mortal wounds,
express empathy with readers both hostile to and in sync with
this poet's basic aims?
Does this poet insult, consciously or unconsciously, the like-minded?
Can it be suggested that she try to prevent this?
If so, what form would the suggestion take?
Since something is to be accomplished, is it necessary
that she have "friends"?

Can these "friends" suggest judicious choices regarding
the density of a center,
and the successful deploying all "ghost words" cleverly
from that center?
Can they suggest that this poet's center pragmatically oversee all
"ghost word operations," successfully managing antithetical stimuli
so that these stimuli push the poet's ideology forward effectively,
without giving offense, so that nothing
remains unfurthered?

How do these ideas identify as "friends"?
Especially as relating to a fraught past (if any; this has not yet been determined).
Would a clear-cut ideology of friends allow words to accrue
(naturally or unnaturally) to actual facts?
Can these ideas-as-friends-as-facts successfully riverboat all ideologies
without exception, and additionally, with appropriate breadth, purity

and sustaining power,
affirm that the poet's innate enmities will not froth continually forth against
her principle expression?

In spite of these innate enmities, does this poet manage to find, express,
and celebrate a faith?
And if so, what is that faith?
Can the faith be expressed succinctly, gracefully in dependable,
forward-moving time?
Or is it a "faith" counter to the essential principles of forward-moving time?
Does the "faith" question chronos? Elevate kairos?
If no, or if so, how does the poet correct this corruption?
Indeed, does she even successfully express this kind of dichotomy
as a corruption?

Is this poet "successful"?
Is this poet "beautiful"?
Does this poet express "value"?
Does she acquiesce sufficiently to the low,
defer appropriately to the high?
Reflect precise cognizance of her station?
Does this poet actively elicit admiration,
or passively attract by innuendo, association?
Does she "housekeep" properly,
clearing chaff before incorporating wheat?
Are those fragrant boughs on her threshold?
Do those boughs "add value"?

Does this poet engage in a nonlocated, disembodied spiritual ethos,
providing little or no solutions to our lives' demands?
Is this her way of expressing—indeed experiencing—
states of mind that are exceedingly seductive, even addictive?
Is this poet "addicted"?
And, if so, is she successfully "addicted"?

Will this poet move politely beyond what is required?
Or will she "showboat?" "Crow?" "Grandstand?" "Badger?" "Preen"?
Can she express her excess per established mainstream conventions?
If no, how might she ultimately assert containment/control?
And will she add normative, recognizable value to that control?
If so, does her work let slip the idea that she believes that control
to be "beautiful"?

Does this poet "woo" you with a restrained enticement?
Or does she draw you in, potential compeer, by enticing with
a practiced, crafted insouciance?
Is this poet lying to/using/exploiting you?
Is she asking too much of her interlocutor, her responder?
Or is her interlocutor/responder projecting personal issues neither contained
nor addressed by the poet,
but rather issues related to, for example, an untended relationship
with a needy parent?

Does this poet bring something—anything—into the light?
And is this light a fair trope that can be described, pointed to, aimed at?
Would you say that the phrase "omnia quae sunt, lumina sunt"
is a valid assessment of the light's role vis-à-vis the poet?
Does the poet know how to protect this light if the light feels
it lies unprotected as it has not yet come into its time?
Does the light exit the precincts of the poet insulted?
Why has the poet violated the light's role?
Does the poet believe that insulting her (admittedly) chosen, fair trope of light
adds normative, recognizable value?
Can these missteps—if indeed they be missteps—
be successfully corrected?

Does this poet have the ability to gracefully deploy rigid structure
as a form of surface-tension release?
Can she "mirror" or effectively deal with opposition?
Does she obstruct, go against, stand up to, the general flow?

What is her position with regard to the flow?
(And the flow's position regarding the poet?)
Is there a standoff?
Is the standoff obstinate? Flawed?
Or a necessary enhancement of value?
Can the standoff be pressed upon to yield?
Or should this poet ultimately be forced to release the standoff
through a faux-relaxed structure plan, attainable within, say,
three or four stanzaic elements?
And can the standoff be asked to track changes
in the poet's will to change?
Is the will to change too much to expect of this poet?
Does this poet exhibit a will to change?

Will this poet ever achieve normative, recognizable value?
Will she someday "seed" her meanings successfully?
Is she fated to always become overly entangled with something/someone?
Can she learn to remain integrated within her own context,
either by the subtle hand of craftsmanship
or strenuous slave-master boundary effort?

Is the life of this poet already delimited?
From where does she get her nutrition?
How does she express conversion from the raw to the cooked,
vulgar to sacrosanct?
Has she ever genuflected, bestowed roses?

How does this poet express discernment, gradual development, maturity?
Has she expended her energy too soon?
Is her natural exuberance completely shot?
What happened to her original radiance, her abundance overflowing?
What complications dictated her choice of dog?
What complications were the result?

Did this poet express her goals too intensely?
Did she standardise?
Did she fail to express empathy?
Did she not successfully protect a soft core by fronting a hard exterior?
If so, has this poet "failed"?

Did this poet ever, at any point, "get it right?"
And if she does, does she do so by engaging in focused, framed self-sabotage,
rejecting the work of making things clear,
eschewing her (purported) goal of revealing the roots of foolishness
by gently dispelling the cloud of unknowing?
Despite her flaws, her wrongs, her sins against convention and taste,
can she still cultivate a reader and become, ultimately,
through a "Pontius Pilate's mosquito" sort of notoriety, influential?

Is the value of this poet simply that she enables engagement?
That she demonstrates the capacity to be present and open,
not grasping at or rejecting either presence or the transcendence of presence,
and thus her openness remains (and retains) a natural adjectival sublime?

Should this poet continue to strive for success
despite her aggressive actions against agency,
her obsessive reanimations of highly personal pied moments,
the consistent shifting of her attentions away
from an immediately visible, comprehensible form
to a postponed instress of questionably pleasurable shock?
Should she blame herself for her failure to cause a bear to appear,
her lack of a proper dog?
And if that failure indeed rests upon the lack of a proper dog,
what dog would be the right dog?
From what kennel, if any, would it come?
And can that lack be remedied?
Ultimately, could it be?
In a final assessment, should it be?

TWO

What If Everything Is Really Okay?

What Happens If Your Eyeball Falls out of the Socket?

What happens if your eyeball falls out of the socket?
What if it falls out, rolls on the ground, and no one can find it?
What if this happens while a volcano is erupting
and everyone is being attacked by monkeys?
What if the monkeys are angry because you have distracted them
from punching sharks, and the sharks are mad
'cause they can't punch back,
and now you've got monkeys AND sharks on your ass?
What if all this time you have a four-hour erection?
What if you try to run away, but your erection gets blown off by snipers
atop the Vermont Country Store—will your legs keep going?
What if someone offers you legs, but the legs are from another planet—
should you take them?
What if the legless alien whose legs were stolen suddenly appears
and throws a writhing pile of "sea kittens" on you,
and the "sea kittens" are rabid and faking Parkinson's
for the benefit of the Taliban, now led by Bubbles the Chimp,
angry and depressed since his owner died,
and plus his kindergarten is suing him
(but that's just the way monkeys smell:
like discarded parts of an old McDonald's)
—what do you do?
Do you pray for a miracle?
But what if all miracles turn out to be bogus
because the Catholic Church has taken back all sainthoods
and replaced them with L.L. Bean support cardigans
made from clown vaginas, but as any fucktard knows
clown vaginas are just too fucking frail to support anything but
angry, macho Bichon Frises with titan haircuts,
barking and lunging and going alpha berserk crazy
on Mr. Whipple's wife, Bill Gates,
who is legs up beneath Curly of the Three Stooges,

in boiling vast whirls of voluptuous melancholic sea turtles—
the heat rippling above the macadam,
the cicadas screaming out of the trees,
and the sky like pewter, glaring—
all of which you can't see because your eyeball
has fallen out of the socket
while a volcano is erupting
and everyone is being attacked
by monkeys?

Why Am I Still Angry with William Blake?

Anyone can be angry.
But it takes balls to be angry with William Blake.
It also takes termites.
And echidnas and ants.

Being angry with William Blake
can be "deep" and also magnificently real
and critical.
It's not like being a fan of everything,
because THAT'S easy: like being a fan
of a peanut in the peanut gun
of Elton John, straight-shot into the mouth
of the luminous high priest elephant-bot
who navigates the stringiest runway
in the history of the battle of rabbit sexing.

Being angry with William Blake is to gravitas
what the Beatles were to Darrin Stephens:
Samantha's elephant-bot friend-with-benefits
OR: Hitler's wife in a Prius.
Did you ever see that *Twilight Zone*
where the guy signed a contract
and they cut out his tongue and it wouldn't die,
it just grew and pulsated and gave birth
to baby tongues?
Well, one of those baby tongues
was William Blake's mother.

How can that be so simple? you ask.
Well, I know for a fact that William Blake said,
"Mother Blake, you are too simple.
You have ten children, and all of them are doing drugs together,

tied up to their eyeballs by zombies.
And that is just totally didactic and unworkable."
And then Mother Blake said, "William Blake,
you have an extensive collection of hairnets
in your hamlet, and that's enough
for me to hate you."

Exactly.
If William Blake were ice cream,
he'd be Heath Bar Peanut Butter Jerk Face.

Why Am I Suddenly Too Old for Manwich?

Apply lip gloss and the world suddenly becomes a serving of vegetables!
Doesn't that make you want to run out and grab a big old bowl of Sloppy Joes?

Sure, it happens with an old photograph or a melody: suddenly you're the lone
Manwich/Sloppy Joes dude in a huge, old, greasy kitchen in Boston, with sweat
dripping off your girth on the mangina side . . . WAAAAAAAAY too subtle
to be a great white shark mook.

Why do stars suddenly appear every time I drink beer ? And with them
the 400-year-old shoulder pads of Lady Gaga
and her mad skool camel-toe mooning boasting a not-too-preppy island mood.

Somewhere in the 70s I found hot dogs to be too sweet for my
cans of Manwich—I never knew exactly how close to death I was until
the old-fashioned Heath Bar/Avatar bioshock set in.

Toronto has slowly been replacing all of its ugly old metal garbage bins with
microwaved popcorn: am I just monkeys, or was macaroni and cheese
once considered drugs in Canada?

Thank God I'm not planning any dramatic Manwich scenes.
Anymore.

Why Am I Suddenly Responsible for
John Cougar Mellencamp's Castration Complex?

So, you want to be a rock star but don't have the talent, money or skills?
Just take a look at how Bono's pre-programmed Al Gore blood Passover
unravels the "castrated Jonas Brothers" allusions of Mussolini eating chalupas.
Then you'll understand what it means to be under the influence of Aerosol Jesus,
dilating like a mofo satyr upon a farm of cysts. Back in 1980, Ronald Reagan
painted Jimmy Carter in a garden and deprived him of androgens, opening a huge
soft spot in the previously impenetrable defenses of Scandinavia. It is this spot—
wan and constipated as the Moody Blues, melodic and dripping with emotions—
that inspired the massive fish murder of Congressman Sonny Bono, followed by
a comical theft of 118 minutes of dismembered Taylor Swift. Even Alfred Hitchcock
could never have imagined that. And even when you reach the near insanity
of Bono perched on an angel by a hearing aid store in Dublin, you're still nowhere near
Indiana's John Cougar Mellencamp, poisoned, castrated, shot, and drowned
all in one night by a priest when he was thirteen. Talk about 24/7 dwarf-dark undertones!

Why Am I Suddenly Loving Your Summery Goyish Om?

Life is pretty freaking dull these days: I wake up early, go to work,
come home and buffalo blog. Then I experience your summery goyish om,
and holy peeing game show!—I itch and itch and itch all over and I am totally
on fire what's up I cannot feel my foot I feel it's like ice cream getting beaten up
by giant stars of GOY = the envy of all things Jewish = the pixie dust on PETER PAN!
And because I am a social critic in Korea there is no way any work is getting done
because I am losing myself in internet hockey-blog fame and the boy-honeys
are all over me like a Second Life knowledge base on cheddar Obama, and
the sun is hitting me, and suddenly there's sun all over me, I'm getting
showered in golden sun drops, and I'm the hairiest girl I know
bouncing all over Yogi Berra like a duck on a june bug
like a donkey on a waffle electing Millard Fillmore
for a fifth term to rule the Jewish 1960s
with Ray Charles in Montana.

Why *Can't* I Be the Forlorn Mildew of Dorian Gray?

Hey, god of mold: ever joined your cats in a ménage à trois?
Have you and them ever played hunt-the-fawn at dawn
while penetrating the deep pie-holes of suburban America?
If you want to have gay sex or visit a library, it's probably
your last night to do those things because my brain, which is on
everything including the front porch, has informed me that Dorian Gray
is really just a rare Italian library truck, fueled by the plagues of Egypt.
And now all I want to do is be a stooge from an audience of twelve-year olds,
getting touched by five presidents.
As I was firing up the MC5 just now, I realized I am totally wtf?'d out
by William Kunstler—and what if Limp Bizkit turns out to be
NutraSweet? A holiday for mice-sized swine?
The closeted plausibility of chihuahuas?

Come back, Mickey Rourke!

What If Everything Is Really Okay?

I think it would be okay to ask if everything's okay.
To write a short essay about everything being okay.
To wonder what would happen if we just decide
that everything is okay.

What if we realize that that which has always really sucked,
and all that we are seeing and experiencing right now that really sucks,
is really okay?
All the while still trying to decipher the hidden well-being in flowers,
and the great relationships between us and the flowers, all of us together
on our Great Space Journey Out.

Is this really where I discover that everything is okay?
That all my day's work is through, and if everything is not okay in the end
then it's not the end?
And that everything is always okay in the end?
What about at the end of the rainbow—everything okay there?
Rainbows are just to look at anyway, not to really understand.
Know what? Maybe it's okay if everything doesn't improve pretty soon.
Cultural Genocide, Culture of Death . . .
I'm pretty ordinary at baking in general, but I rock at scones.
And I wasn't really a point guard in high school, but I did ask Magic Johnson
"What is this deepness? Is every day really Christmas?"
And Magic Johnson answered:
"As Gandalf says in *The Lord of the Rings*: 'That's right, amigos—
reality doesn't care what you think or believe.'"
But really, Gandalf was just retweeting the sweet words of Sade's
Super Bowl half-time show: "I'm feeling strangely attracted to snow,
and I'm half-starting to glow."

Everything is cool, Deacon Blues,
except I'm still waiting for my 360° super blintz to get here.

What is a blintz?
Is it a pastry or a food?
Either way, it's okay.
One of the most ecstatic experiences of my life was yesterday
as I crawled across the floor of a famous café called
Outhouse in the Woods.
Try that for a few days or hours,
or better yet, the rest of your life.
Show me a man who is completely present to whatever he is doing,
and I'll show you a woman who is a rotten idol of unconsciousness,
a true revolution AGAINST SOMETHING, obviously,
but merging WITH EVERYTHING.

Many have said that prayer is all that God wants,
but really—is he just strange bunny rabbit poop, or what?
How many people think he's green?
Is God okay?
Dear Eskimo and Sparrow: Is it okay to talk about God being okay
with monkeys at the dinner table?
With Pixar-style animation in the form of a woodpecker
inside a woman's head?
Is God not okay with girl-on-girl kisses?
How about four boys coming together
to change Christian breakdancing . . . forever?
Can Christians use marijuana according to scripture?
Does freedom in Christ allow this?
Instead of asking, "Is it okay for a Christian to get a tattoo,"
ask instead "Why is the stuck-up bitch who created Shawnimals
(the snakelike thing and the puffier thing)
casting evil elves on Vin Diesel?
Will the result be glorifying to God?
Or just more chocolate-covered bacon on a stick?"
(On a stick!)

What I want to talk about now
is not how context is everything,
but why context is everything,
and why everything is okay.
Because apparently Beyoncé has permission from God
to wear hot clothes.
As her booty moves and changes,
making most of us uncomfortable
and uncertain about what may happen next,
God wants us to know that, "Everything will be okay 'cause
that's me, God, doing the moving and the changing.
You don't even have to call me God if you don't want to.
Some call me Jehovah, some call me Mohammed,
some call me Vishnu . . . but I vish they'd stop."
Apparently God must be drunk.
I'm considering staying just a little bit drunk myself from now on.
I am in the South,
where women take nips of potent Eastern European distilled plum brandy
throughout the day, as they sit around being short.
Who am I to argue?
Did God create Da Bears, and make them superior to all teams?

If not, then God is just a hypothesis.
Okay, I stole that from the ancient Sumerians.

Petite words fail when describing the final unfurling of my dream
of Simon Cowell tossing Nikola Tesla's letterhead
to the sharks in his toilet.
But don't worry; everything is okay.
There's no need to act.
Nothing needs to change.
The Love Police hope to wake everyone up
from the real-life Matrix.

My name is Chad Manville,

and I am experiencing the self-sound of the emptiness of dharmata,

which is the sound of a thousand spontaneous thunderbolts.

I am surrounded by various gatekeepers and light-bringers

all of whom are okay with "add to cart."

And yet I am totally fucking with "add to cart!"

And that's okay, too.

Also okay is global super gayness.

So, please, just go about your business.

What Happened to the Women of Country Valley?

I loved the women of Country Valley.
And I know what happened to them.
At least I think I do.

I was a youth back then,
jonesing for a corgi,
and my thoughts of love were long, long thoughts.
At least that's what I think I thought.

It happened when I was on the merry-go-round.
It was an apple-green evening in Country Valley.
There was Susan, gray and faithful handmaiden,
and Miss Cornelia walking briskly along,
and Anne of Green Gables with goo all over—
a gusty group of daffodils on the old, mellow lawn.

They wore shiny space dresses gathered at the ankles
by elastic cuffs which extended over red glowing boots.
On their arms were large silver gauntlets
with flared arm coverings
extending halfway up their forearms.
I was the one they hypnotized.

I looked up and found myself
in a magical spell-weaving place:
the women of Country Valley
had let a highly excited, disobedient boy
loose upon their spaceship.
I don't need hypnosis to recall this.
Memory-erasing methods don't work on me anyway.

Their spaceship looked like the most beautiful Legos,
Legos too beautiful to be made by humans.

It was decorated with fancy menstrual cup pouches
made of antique brocade fabric from Japan.
Miss Cornelia turned to me with a smile and said,
"Can you believe this is just an old RV
that became a Lego spaceship in our minds?"

Then I had the weirdest thought:
"Wouldn't it be something
if the Fonz suddenly appeared?"
The Fonz could yell at Potsie
from the comfort of his spaceship
floating high above the earth!

Then the spaceship lands on the roof of SCTV,
leaves some cabbages, and takes off again!
Come on, who wouldn't want to spend
alien Christmas with the Fonz
on a spaceship hiding behind the Hale–Bopp comet?
Maybe then all the mysteries would be solved,
like how come that *Footloose* dude
never actually cut loose?

Then something bad happened:
a horde of evil monsters that looked like Flipper
rampaged down the peaceful mountains
led by evil Uncle Unicorn
who had the frightful ability to deliver swift flying kicks.
Anne of Green Gables got kicked first
and I cried, "Damn you with all the speed of the red bruschetta
that Geddy Lee's mother gave him!"

I swear to god, if I was Jesus,
I would have killed that unicorn every time he directed
an episode of *The A-Team*.

All I would've needed was Anna-Nicole's dead body,
many sixes of Genesee Cream Ale,
and a Bard College sweatshirt from the college bookstore.

But then the Fonz really did appear!
With his army of anthropomorphic ducks
who fight aliens in T-shirts that say Milwaukee to Bronze the Fonz!
It was the highest level of mutancy
that someone as sensitive as the Fonz could achieve.
How potent was the Fonz in combat?
No god in the world could've beaten the Fonz.

I'm in Seattle right now, in a youth hostel,
sitting in a room crying.
The Army doesn't want anyone
to know what really happened.
Why must the Fonz
continue to be denied any type of fame?
Since nothing will be done about this
at the government level,
I guess we really will have to
defend the Fonz ourselves.

I don't live in Country Valley anymore.
I live in Silicon Valley.
Um, no I don't; I live in Florida.
Okay, I live behind Emu Mountain
in a cabin made completely of emus.
But I still love the women of Country Valley.
I think I always will.
At least that's what I think I think.

Assemblage, Moeity, Propinquity

Assemblage, Moeity, Propinquity

A boy and a girl, both violet-eyed, insouciant, with incipient wings, sitting by a chimney.

The girl with violet eyes and incipient wings, in love with a beleaguered, brooding boy with carved-rock cheekbones.

The brooding boy with carved-rock cheekbones—lissome, sweet, summery—in love with a girl penumbral in color, mellow and super happy in a bungalow.

The mellow girl penumbral in color, in love with a bucolic boy who lithely jumped off a bus after a young gazelle and got hit with a tranq bullet.

The bucolic boy who, after recovering from getting hit with the tranq bullet, fell in love with a fetching ingénue—umbrella haircut, eyes chatoyant—who strode unhindered in opulence toward a perfect good.

The fetching ingénue who strode in opulence toward a perfect good because she was in reality moving in unison with a furtive, comely boy twerking it to the future between two moonlit lagoons.

The comely boy who, while twerking it to the future between the two lagoons, became inured to an imbroglio involving alien cyborgs in the offing and his lifelong nemesis: a boy sporting a gossamer 'fro of mysterious abilities and cheeks efflorescent with joy—his secret cynosure.

The boy whose cheeks are efflorescent with joy because he is beside his beloved girl-cousin Dalliance as she chooses, with forbearance, from a plethora of magical tools and talismans, one of which—the Shield of Desuetude—she must use to dissemble an evil, ineffable destiny.

The girl named Dalliance who experiences an epiphany and chooses correctly the Shield of Desuetude and so produces a boon for humanity, and then, as part of the panacea, asks a demure boy named Halcyon (his burlappy dreadlocks wafting an evocative petrichor and swinging like rope around his shoulders), "What is the felicity of this harbinger Earth, this redolent green seraglio moored in the stars, and of the Moon which lilts the air like a susurrus evanescence, so soon to unravel, and with what stars has God imbued this night, and why?"

The demure boy with dreadlocks who trails a length of diaphanous petunias tucked into his underpants, at the end of which sits his pet fungal onion, Susquehanna, in love with a tiny pony with a vestigial head hanging languorously from its neck, a head that is, in reality the woebegone ghost of some erstwhile Surrealist.

And the woebegone ghost of this erstwhile Surrealist, in a previous life one ingredient in a bitter elixir but in this one nothing more than a fugacious mote, the least scintilla of a long-lost palimpsest, but whose mote-love is the emollient ripple in the ether that suspires a wish in the heart of all things to bring the violet-eyed boy and a girl, insouciant, with incipient wings, to configure in miraculous imbrication by a chimney.

THREE

Someday We Shall All Say Yes to Death

A Unicorn Boner for Humanity

You, sir or madame, are a nazi
if you deny the unicorn-humanity
of those of us less fortunate
in the beauty department.

When I first published *The Unnatural State of the Unicorn*
in Polish, unicorns were strangers to mankind,
dwelt far away from humanity,
seeking out mountains, forests,
places where magic might still be found.
They ran through green woodlands,
proud and free,
never chased by greedy humanity.

Kids these days
with their rap music and boners
are going to eradicate humanity.
(Keep in mind that I have no idea
how children are made.)

The discretion, the honesty,
and the humanity of the unicorn boner—
if I could change anything about myself,
I would have a unicorn boner in my mouth
two days ago, and by 212 people total.

How empty is a world without rainbows!
Where would we be without unicorns!
"Every day I feel a little more horny"
is clearly a nod to the unicorn boner—
solidarity with all things happy and fluffy
and horny.

As pink, as new, and as loud
as a newborn unicorn boner.
And when you follow your newborn unicorn boner,
boners will occur where you would not have thought there were boners,
and where there wouldn't be boners for anyone else.

There's gonna be lots of moist newborn unicorn boner verbalizing
in somebody's vajayjay.

Just you watch.

The Swiss Just Do Whatever

The Swiss just do whatever
like masturbating their doink-doinks
deep in rural France
in the shadow of Mont Blanc.

Heavy, dependable
and prepared for whatever,
the Swiss vaginal simulacrum recognizes
(as potential for larder)

King Hussein and President Fabio,
always just about to touch each other
on their devolved sparkle-offs
and Neil Patrick Harris appreciation pages.

Everyone knows when these bizarre Swiss cometh
they cometh with fluffy Beatles-like
six packs of shit-covered reindeer
knock-knocking like a bummer.

Glitter is the Swiss Army knife
of the most bedazzlingly ridiculous
emotions: the part just before
the paranoid cheesemaker says:

"Whatever you do in Palm Springs,
don't yodel"—a most unusual Swiss Miss
mixture of very early skunk and the robotic
sadness of women's mold:

heavy, greasy, dense and low, like
lethargic sea-green gardens

with a buzz overpowering, like
modern outdoor inbreeding.

You know you're Swiss
when foreign visitors ask to see your
chocolate factory and you answer,
"Why don't you and Hannibal Lecter

just kick out the jams?"
'Cause you know you got the chamber,
the chair, and *Fear Factor*.

Someday We Shall All Say Yes to Death

This isn't about big tent show business.
This isn't about the saddest of carnivals.
This isn't about the last time real TV had a decent show.
This is about how good Life and Death go together.

This is about how someday we shall all say yes to Death.

Yes, someday we shall all say yes to Death,
which is not the same as someday saying yes to
being Death Cab for Cutie's ugly groupie.
Yes, Gabriel will sound that trumpet and it's pin curls,
Noxzema and Phyllis-Diller face
for three million eternities.

Yes, someday we shall collapse upon ourselves
and form a glistening star in a collision of galaxies
that includes three-dimensional fractal globules
floating close to each other in linear sequence.
Together with Death we shall be
twin panda supernovas orbiting the vast disembodied
consciousness of Oprah.
But until then where would we be if we gave up
our dreams of partying with piñatas
and joined some German emo army?

Oh, yes, Chachi, oh, yes: we shall groan and sigh,
we shall bitch about children, cosmetics, and doing the dishes,
but this is only the groan of persistent existence.
This is only the groan of "Well, if there *is* a resurrection of the body,
then what will we live in when we're dead?"
This is the groan of, "Oh thanks, dead Gilligan,
for making it with Kentucky's second-biggest jackass mascot

on television."
Oh yes, we groan and sigh.
But can we just say yes
to the winnowing fingers, the fins and wings
that rock the shimmering dust mote swirl?
To the miracle of cells that stiffen into an expensive blond wood
of unicorn endurance?
If I have the stomach for being gossiped about by Gary Numan
in Tucson at a barbeque
can I also accept the plush velvet panic room
full of mini Charles Mansons
that is Death's little piñata party?
When wiped down it occasionally
makes little cooing sounds.
If your ideas about death are set in concrete,
or if your heart is not open to unusual intrusions,
please stop dying right now.
That's right—you can't.

Can you imagine how different our country would be
if no one was afraid of death?
I dream of the appreciation for time-as-ocean,
with all things past, present and future
discernible by the sun, which has no choice
but to shine on everyone.

So yes, I shall say yes to Death,
to Death's 70s seersucker gaucho pants in orbit,
its promotional nature
in which we become collectible dolls of a moon goddess
floating between worlds as a shrine to shirts
of disembodied threshold births.
When conditions are sufficient,
there is a manifestation.
And when we meet again

in other forms, introduced as friends,
will we still be each other's #1 drumming bee priestesses?
Creatures with antennae are special.
Homunculi are extra special.
Extra extra special is Death,
the wicked pink unicorn
to which we say yes.

When Kitties Kill Babies

You may think that because God loves to kill babies,
it doesn't give kitties permission to kill babies.
But do you realize that an angry kitty would kill you
and everyone you love?
"Kill the Babies! Kill them!!!" screams the tiny angry kitty,
driving an ambulance over the speed limit
and running over babies.

Abortions don't kill babies.
Unaborted kitty babies kill babies.
We have a new onesie design in Ye Olde Zazzle Shoppe this afternoon,
courtesy of our beloved Bronco Jew Drywall:
"Jewish Kitties Can Kill Gentile Babies Who Threaten Israel . . .
Much to Ron Paul's Dismay."

Babies who kill kitties make this rapper confused,
but kitties who kill babies redefine caregiving.
The quest to explore the kitty-killers phenomenon led researchers
to build this utterly terrifying baby robot
which kills babies before the baby-killing kitties get to them.
I was on the fence about supporting the violent baby-building movement,
but here's something to celebrate:

500,000 baby-killing kitties have been let loose in Rome
because Obama tweeted "Kitties killing babies—Yes we can!"
Their little twats can pulverize planets! Oooh, look
at the cute little babies. Cute nothin'—
they're dead!"

If you're a human and you kill babies, you're a monster.
But if you're a cute angry kitty who kills babies,
it's just the right thing to do.

If I Could Marry Meat

If I could marry meat
I would marry pig faces, pig ears,
cow feet & the biggest slab of
Hispanic shopper ever.
Who doesn't want to marry that?
Blood & raw meat
and flies landing everywhere.
What else would I marry?
The maggoty meat scene from
Battleship Potemkin
goat head & lamb organs
& "flap meat"
(looks like something out of
The Flintstones).
You know how I would marry meat?
Get super fit with Spider Man
and smear it on the wall.
Bridesmaids would be
bacon bras & hot dog rakes.
Maid of honor:
deer antler candy.
Best man, either raw yak
or horse-meat ham.
Maybe even jerky-flavored George W. Bush.
I see you all salivating over there.
All normal people want to marry meat.
Even Dutch people want to marry meat.
If I went to a barbeque & there was no meat,
I would say, "Today, me & Spider Man
will rip you humans apart like helpless worm fungus!"
Excuse the bear poop in the beginning;
I messed up.

But you know what's damn sexy?
Star Trek mirror-meat episodes,
Mila Kunis being Ukrainian for the Meat Olympics,
and the meat-based lifestyle of Mrs. Wheelbarrow
on regular-ass TV.
And all that mad cow going around.
Man, I gotta go.
I gotta go marry me some meat.
I'm gonna go marry me some duck tongue.
And then I'm gonna sit back and watch all you goddamn honky haters
put on your boogie shoes.

Did You Forget This Is the Zombie Dick Apocalypse?

You are just too stupid to live if you can straight-facedly ask
"Was there a Zombie Dick Apocalypse that I was unaware of?"
DUH!
It was facilitated through Manichean rhetoric on the rhizomes
during the previous Zombie Dick Apocalypse
when Urizen fell weeping from heaven and poured snow
on lucid dreaming Ryan Seacrest.
That's pretty much the way Christianity works in Denmark.

I feel about the Zombie Dick Apocalypse much like an Irish American feels about
the ball declanking ointment known as Hebrew school that includes
a pious Hindu from Lucknow who doesn't believe in alien abductions
and David Crosby helplessly hoping for someone
to buy his cherished sailboat, the *Little Keith Richards*.
What do David Crosby, Bank of America
and the University of Connecticut have in common?
Misguided outrage over Hoboken's cheesy version of the Zombie Dick Apocalypse:
Zombie Dick Van Dyke Apocalypse.

Overheard during the real Zombie Dick Apocalypse:

White boy #1:   Dewd, I'm totally betting my pizza money on
                 Captain Ahab McGay's 69 dude pants!

White boy #2:   Level 96 tank-mages are strong but they're no
                 captain 69 dude pants.

Predictions for the next Zombie Dick Apocalypse:

Sexy Hair
Dying Owls
Blood

Hoodies
Mustaches
Zelda Fitzgerald
  (as Zombie Dick Eliminator)

Pimp My Top-Kill Live-Feed Mothership

Pimp my Top-Kill Live-Feed Mothership
Pimp it with a legendary Saddam relationship
Pimp it with three-day throttle like a pimp beats a whore
Pimp it fast with patches of dry skin from Chris Matthews
'cause pretty soon nobody's gonna care

Pimp BP's little portapotty mistake with the
Top Kill Live Feed posing for Playboy
'cause this spill is already pimp!
Pimp the dead Cajun way of life with flava attainment, swankienda style:
with a disco ball in a Top-Kill Live Feed club with a laser!
Poor people can always dance

Pimp me some CEO martyrdom as a last stand for pussies
who can't honestly kill a man so they remotely soak a pelican
Pimp me every second of Rick Warren and associate pastors singing "Brick House"
'cause they think the world needs more "Brick House"-singing
than it does Top Kill Live Feed-bringing

Pimp me some wiki-educated bitch keepin' it real:
"I would prefer to be Jackson 5'ed by Steve Jobs than hear about some new
boring ocean problem . . .
in other words: pimp me pimping a snake
being weaned from your balls"

Pimp that minute fraction of a second when you realize you just made a huge mistake,
and so you super pimp "Pimp My Lotto, Super Jesus!"
to poor people via "supply-side economics"
in order to pimp the super endangered nacho pimp hand of celebutainment

(BTW, aren't the oceans already dead?)

This Gorilla Called Philip Sidney

Miss Pamela ♀ (the Aunt of Fear)
invented the Elizabethan poet Sir Philip Sidney,
in whose cottage are found invisible clues to the sources
of Ted Nugent, wicked aboriginal stepmother
of Sir Philip Sidney.

This gorilla called Philip Sidney,
keeper of the shared surprise
of running naked through the Gorilla House,
wants to prove he can bring Uncle Esperanto
back from the dead.
I hear squirrels talking about this.

The 800-Pound Gorilla in the Room—
a Jewish Philip Sidney biting his own "truant penis"
("look in thy heart / and expect / a 600-pound
truant penis")—
passes Voldemort parmesan
in the shadows where I ruined my life,
then clawed my way back through 108
pig-hearted sonnets to my old familiar
dick-to-mouth existence.

One thing that I teach all my composition students
is that the gorilla promotion code is always
"Philip Sidney Is Vienna's Answer to Hash Browns,
Congo the Chimp Is Back in the Art World,
and You Have Zero Facts."
—Philip Sidney, at the top of a tent pole,
scratching himself like a gorilla
in all his "nature places."

The smell shall haunt me
to the end of days.

You're a Buttfaced Joni Mitchell

Hey there, Doggie! You got a funny bunny buttface
and a dark cloud above you—you're a
modern day Joni Mitchell Klingon Supernova,

not even approaching Stevie Nicks v.2, late Janis,
or anytime Rihanna—'cause while Taylor Swift is
just some lipstick, Joni is the lezbohemian mascot

of Canada, dirty for dirty. Um, wait—
forget Canada! You are such a totally born-dead
Emily "I Live on Dread" Dickinson anxiety exhibit

that Orrin Hatch found shit flies on your qwerty . . .
and then Paul Bunyan killed and ate them, apropos
giant stag monster Joni, all "canon" and "classic"

and "buttfaced."

Are you messing with Joni at daycare again?
I will be calling anyone who messes with Joni at
daycare "Buttface McBallnuts" from now on,

'cause what do you think this is, a *Wonder Years*
transcript written by the alternate tunings of
Breakfast Barney's (Pat Metheny's) sign-off prayer?

On the other hand, how much do I LOVE that you
think Ween's chick factor is just some secret banjo
crap? But how much do I HATE when Li'l Jewish Anxiety

(lame trippin' booty hero) meets Dead Joni Society
at the petting zoo? But how much do I LOVE
that this is the best season of Wong Fu weekends

in Not-Fucking-Canada ever?!

My Name in Hebrew

My Hebrew-speaking friends
tell me that my name in Hebrew
means "poet or lyricist."
Also "poet or lyricist with insomnia,"
sometimes "psalmist with insomnia,"
and at other times "one who feeds her cats insomnia today
and tomorrow pills made from dead babies
and insomnia."
One particular Hebrew-speaking friend
(whose own name means "eat Al Gore and you'll get anorexia")
tells me that my name in Hebrew might also mean
"your portly psychiatrist is unnerved by your project involving
all the baldness of Hollywood's insomnia."
In fact, in a recent episode of
My Revenant Mama Eats Your Mama's Insomnia,
starring three of my Hebrew-speaking friends,
all with Hollywood insomnia,
both the donkey cart and the donkey
are related to the King of Trainee Retinas
and afflicted with insomnia.
And in order to lull him into
Breathing New Life into the Zombie Apocalypse
they use the Jewish revenge-fantasy aspect of
Inglourious Basterds—thousands of Tel Aviv children singing
a doo-wop version of "The Binding of Isaac" from Genesis 22,
in which God falls ill in February 1603
and commands Isaac's father in Pig Latin to
"ab-stay your un-say and then am-scray."
But "God's insomnia" can also be Hebrew code for
"full of rage in one of NYU's mole tunnels
with a goatee full of toxic angora."
So what am I supposed to believe?

Especially when scientists at Purdue's Hebrew University in Mahwah, Jerusalem
are breathing new life into the menacing running zombie
that is not merely a revenant but a rageful, rabid
cab-driving mime hobbit with eczema,
drunk on sixteen Insomnia-bin-Ladens
every day before lunch.
I have no choice but to believe that,
like the New Zealand volcano in *The Lord of the Rings*,
I should be taking the marijuana pills
supplied by my greengrocer
to beat insomnia.
And then maybe my Hebrew name will be
"your orgy goons are ruining my community musical about
Fall Out Boy's archival Dacwoo with their kebab acne
(and insomnia)."

A Wedding Song

A wedding song!
The bridegroom is coming!
The equal of Ares,
much bigger than a big man and nobody,
and I mean nobody—
not even the rain—
has such small hands.

As for the bride, she scatters
a thousand fragrant posies!
Whole beds of roses!
Also penguin dust,
werewolf bathtubs, radiant brains,
a bag of broken Bach records,
the heaviest nuns,
that stuff on unwashed vegetables
and a cat shovel.
Her gown is of the finest wool,
with a belt of straw and ivy buds,
from which pretty lambs we pull,
because those lambs are really making her uncomfortable,
and that belt of straw sucks, too,
and why is she wearing wool in August anyway?
Does she have a thing for sheep or what?
And so we, the wedding guests,
some in bed sheets, some in blouses,
some in smocks, all rising together in calm swells
of halcyon feeling, filling whatever we wear
with the deep joy of our impersonal breathing,
and of course with the lambs we pulled—
some safely hidden in our blouses, some in our smocks
most in our bed sheets—

because otherwise those crazy lambs would be running
all over the place
eating all the cake
and going to the bathroom on the rugs.

Now they are flying in place—
the bride and groom, not the lambs—
conveying the terrible speed of their omnipresence.
And now of a sudden
they swoon down into so rapt a quiet
that nobody seems to be there.

But that's because nobody is there,
but then we return quickly to our seats,
lambs safely constrained in bed sheets.
And the hotel's vaguely Christian officiant says, "You were born together,
and together you shall be forevermore.
You shall be together when the white wing of death
dances between you like a fat Reichian wife
screeching over potatoes 'Get a job!'
You probably won't have to worry about potatoes though, so
give one another of your bread, but not from the same loaf,
because you never know about mold, but then again
wasn't ergotism the basis for the visions of eighteenth-century Hasidic *zaddiq*
Nachman of Bratslav? The ancient Greek Eleusinian Mystery cults?
And that gaggle of Hollywood boys hiring poor Russian girls to swallow
loaves of bread up their anuses, as the sun acknowledges with a warm look
the world's hunks? How does that work? No, really, I'm asking.
Okay, okay, not appropriate. Anyway, if these pleasures may thee move,
then let shepherds' swains dance and sing!
Let there be clean linen for the backs of thieves!
Let there be nothing on earth but laundry!"
And then the bride says, "I love you as a sheriff searches for a walnut!"
And the groom says, "I love thee freely, as men strive for a walnut!"
And the bride says, "In your most frail gesture are things which enclose me!"

And the groom says, "So when are you going to stop people killing whales?"
And we, with squirmy lambs embedded in our bosoms, cry,
"My hopped-up husband drops his home disputes,
and hits the streets to cruise for prostitutes!"
And in our eyes you can see some obscene honeymoon going on.

At the reception, after tea and homemade cookies,
our astounded souls,
bereft of 2000 years and a bath,
hang for a moment bodiless and simple, hoping
there's going to be more than just freakin' tea and cookies—
the invitation said gluten-free beef, wtf?
Outside the hotel window,
where the air is all awash with angels,
and where Christ's flaming halo revolves forever
(he is the lovely lily we all worship,
he is the red-haired torch no wind may blow out
Christ who flies higher than the aviators
and holds the world's record),
the bride and groom cavort.
Like a mighty wind they raise to heaven their voices in song:
harmonious thunderings like the seats of heaven among
a second sharknado of the poor:

"Now I am quietly waiting for the catastrophe of your love for yoghurt,"
the bride sings.

"I would rather look at you," the groom yodels, "than all the portraits in the world
except possibly for the Polish Rider occasionally and anyway it's in the Frick
which thank heavens you haven't gone to yet."

But it turns out that wasn't just a literary trope sharknado
but a "real" one,
and so now the bride and groom stride alone through the Paris crowds,
buses in bellowing herds roll by,

and anguish clutches their throats
because they are horrified at finding themselves suddenly in Paris
because of a sharknado.
And the bride cries, "The sharknado almost drowned me in Montmartre!"
And the groom replies, "The sharknado is like my love—
a shameful disease."
Terrified they see in the depths of the Seine a giant squid
and then feel better because it's a familiar, flarfy symbol
gliding through seaweed.
Next they are in a tavern garden near Prague
watching a rosebug asleep in a rose's heart.
Then in Marseilles among piles of watermelons.
Then in Coblenz at the Giant's hotel.
And in Rome sitting under a Japanese tree,
and in Amsterdam with a girl they find pretty but who is ugly.
Turns out it's an international sharknado.

Surprisingly though, none of us are harmed, and so meanwhile we,
the wedding guests,
fall gracelessly into the hotel elevators,
because now that the bride and groom have disappeared,
and those damn lambs are finally asleep between the arbor vitae
outside the hotel,
we're all going to do the same thing tonight:
run rampant into those almost climactic suites!
Hordes of us! Husbands! Wives! Flowers! Chocolates!
The indifferent clerk he knowing what's going to happen,
the lobby zombies they knowing what,
the whistling elevator man knowing,
everybody knowing . . .
it's almost like we're getting married ourselves—all of us!
Running rampant and yelling Radio Belly! Blue Cross!
Gas & Electric! Knights of Columbus!
Ah, here finally is our cup of flowers and our kirtle,
our black velvety jackets of brilliant flies which buzz around cruel smells,

the pee stains on our underwear . . .
talk about the woe that is in marriage!
From other rooms we hear the barbaric yawps of our fellow guests
as we stall above each other like elephants:
"I know the skies bursting with lightning, and the waterspouts!"

"I have seen the low sun spotted with unknown saps resembling actors on very ancient soap operas viewable only on YouTube! I want you to scream, 'Fuck me, Chad Manville!'"

"I have dreamed I followed pregnant and hysterical cows, mingling with panthers' eyes and human skin!"

"I have seen a whole Leviathan rotting in the rushes! Avalanches of water in the midst of the recent nuptials of Kimye cataracting toward the abyss!"

"Come live with me and give it up! I was a star for Mineola Prep!"

Oh, the hordes of us! The flowers and the chocolates and the kirtles and the cups! Oh, Gas & Electric! Oh, Knights of Columbus!

Someone's going to stay until the cows come home
or my name isn't Frank O'Hara!

Oh, wait. It's not.

Our Celebrities, Our Celebrity Cheese™

The more corrupt our country gets
the more we love Our Celebrities—
their jobs, their haircuts,
their money.
One year is as another,
and it becomes hard to remember
even the death of one's own mother
when Nicole Kidman's Botox issues
stand firmly in the way.

Let's face it: we hate Our Fat People,
but we love Our Celebrities.
Posh Spice's love life
is more on our daughters' minds than dolls are,
and every damn day
Brangelina dies a little for our sins.
Yea, though I be surrounded by despair,
I shall not let it engulf me,
for you shall take my sufferings from me
George Clooney
with your gentle hands.
The darkest and harshest of life's events
are simply mysteries of gentle benevolence.
Hasn't Christina Aguilera ministered to this?

When Our Celebrities heard that England
was at the bottom of the European Tree League
they sprung into action with five thousand pounds
of nutrient-rich goo sealed in lard
and swirling with bacteria.
That's how Celebrity Cheese™ was created.
Celebrity Cheese™ has become the most important

of all celebrity cheeses
in the post-Diana celebrity cheesemaking genre.
Celebrity Cheese™ is milk's leap toward immortality.
And somewhere in the world today
lives a Celebrity Cheese Child™
who will change everything.

Our Celebrities are regularly asked,
"Do you make and eat your own cheese?"
Whitney Houston, for example,
packages and finishes her own cheese logs.
And Robin Gibb wants Bulgarian sheep milk cheese
in his dressing room on the day of his concert.

What cheeses would you like to see
in Celebrity Cheese™?
What cheeses would you like to see
in Celebrity Cheese Deathmatch™?

Today I got calls from David Bowie,
Melanie Griffith
and Celebrity Cheese™.
Whose do you think I answered first?

With their basic human themes,
Our Celebrities are one of our most powerful
and personal ways of working out
what we feel about celebrity.
And cheese.

So let's cozy up in celebrity style,
in love with every living being in the universe.
Let's take a good look at Alec Baldwin's chart
to better understand why he would mouth off at his kid.
Yes, there is a lot wrong with this picture.

But I think you'll understand that if I suddenly slip into
my dirty ballerina flats and stained sweater
it's only because I love Jennifer Garner.
I love her and Victor Garber.
I love her and Ben Affleck together.

What is my message?
That we are living in the Great Celebrity Days,
so let's hold ourselves to that power that gathers
on the celebrity side of transcendence.
Let's drink our fill of love till morning.
Let's gorge ourselves on terrible perfect apples.
And let's accessorize!
Because the ability to accessorize
is what separates us from noncelebrities.
And cheese.

When the Moon Turned Away

I looked at the moon, and the moon turned away.
I looked at the moon on the water,
and the water turned away.
At least it should have been the moon, or the water,
but those shapes on the water were just the landmasses of Asia,
turning away.
I looked below me and the grasses looked up afraid
in a sick green light
at the moon which had turned away.
The moon was too small anyway, to give much light.
Maybe it was sorry for hitting me that time.
Maybe it was sorry that I turned away.
Maybe it never saw the pain that made me turn away.
I was a moon once, too.
A singing moon.
A bright smiling moon with a baby truth.
A white seesaw baby bouncing up and down.
Look up, all of you.
Come on look up because I am still the moon
and beautiful
in the rearview mirror,
like a woman
not salt-bound, not sad,
not a ghost caught crying.
At least not that.

Build This Chariot

Build this chariot.
Build it now.
Build it with a syrinx
redolent of poppers.
Build it by flooding
the Continental Hem
with vino tinto
and bacalao.
Flood it now.
Flood it with shredded
clinic morsels
in a basket
appropriated from its original
clock-out function
as you clock-out shredding,
shredding now.
Your name is Cloud
you farm a cow
in fields rife with horses.
You wipe your mouth
a lot—you cup.
You run hard
go long with hits
in a wild west
giggling and ratcheting
and releasing weevils
built of bricks.
Thickset and generous,
your brick nuts activate
the nuts inside
my woodwork
which I dap beside you,

I dap there now.
'Cause I aim to come
correct
siphon the derelict
chamber with looting
as I lope.
Because it's a perimeter.
It's a mitzvah,
when building strips come
incessant with bulbs
and strange wading
and building
and more building
and we together
build this chariot
build it strong
and strange
with necks
and squeaks
and flood it with shredded
clinic morsels.
We build this chariot.
We build it now.

Anything in the Sky Is Probably a Golden Human Woman with Kitten Hands

Cowboy little match girls—
oracles of evening
and caretakers of leaves—
stalk the green grass
in a red coral ring.
Their destination,
the plain, heavyweight
substance of keepsakes—
a radiance which was
once so bright.

I hide from them,
but they find me again:
leaning on a mailbox,
eating a green apple,
advancing my own aims
in shabby hand-me-downs.
They find me again,
and set me on this path.
And I must move, clutching my books
of chance events and encounters
of euphemisms and taboos,
my books made of bark.
They were always
at my heels,
brandishing their souvenirs of the worst
of the six afflictions,
their hurting memories
like sharp-shinned birds.
Once more they force me to be
the one living presence
on the concourse; everyone else,

already dead.
They speak with a voice
of three antique maps.
They are the ones to whom I am
truly grateful.

Together we push toward
some foreign source
of sacrifice—
the lime of starfish
in a Florida room—
together we climb the blue bones
of a loathsome body
overprotected by heavy flesh.
This body is a portal to more
azure paths, and finally we enter
an immensity of sweaters.
Here is where the plain, heavyweight
keepsakes fade.
Here is where
I lose the sky.
Here is where
they smile:
"Everything serves to further,"
they say.

This millennium of sun is so
unforgiving—like a scattered array
of constellations crawling
with the stink of saints.
Probably the earliest universe
was nothing more than a flyswatter
made of dirt and nectarines
with a massive set of jaws
and teeth that sprouted around gills.

Anything in the sky was probably
a golden human woman
with kitten hands.

Here is where
I lose the sky.
There is no finish line.
No loving cup,
no body crown,
no banners waving
from a balustrade.
Here is where
I say goodbye:
a blur of feathered epaulets.
Here is my dinner
of lizards.
These bells?
Just televisions
in the mist.

Notes

I Know Well the #1 Thing Keeping Me from Really Learning How to Knit Is My Own Deep Inner Shrug is for Becca Klaver.

This Poet is for Edwin Torres, adapted from Chris Lofting's writings on the *I Ching*.

Why Am I Suddenly Loving Your Summery Goyish Om is for Benjamin Bourlier.

Assemblage, Moeity, Propinquity contains a selection of the "fifty most beautiful words in the English language."

You're a Buttfaced Joni Mitchell is for Jenna Briedis.

A Wedding Song is for Brooke Michelle Robison and K. Silem Mohammad, after Sappho, Shakespeare, Marlowe, Corso, Cummings, Browning, Wilbur, Blake, Apollinaire, O'Hara, Gibran, Rimbaud, Koch, and Anderson (Pamela).

Build This Chariot is for Alli Warren.

Acknowledgments

This book was made possible through generous grants of friendship, good humor and support—especially during a very difficult time—from Shanna Compton, Joanna Fuhrman, Boni Joi, Nada Gordon, Drew Gardner, Katie Degentesh, Kasey Mohammad, Gary Sullivan, Edwin Torres, Elisabeth Workman, Marjorie Shaxted, Paul Hoover, Fork Burke, Kathleen Ossip, Shamar Hill, Jennifer L. Knox, Joel Lewis, Dominic Wroblewski, Deborah Pintonelli, Robert Viscusi, Christina Woodbury, Christopher Eaves, Jack Hanley, Patricia Messmer, Michele Somerville, John Guzlowski, Sharon Paradise, Ron Kolm, Daniel Nester, Francesco Levato, Luis Jaramillo, Laura Cronk, Lori-Lynn Turner, Justin Sherwood, Gregory Collins, John Reed, and Deborah Landau. Nicholas Jackowiak, you are a miracle in my life. David Borchart, I love you more than words can tell.

My sincere thanks to the editors of the following publications, blogs and websites in/ on which some of these poems first appeared. My sincerest apologies to anyone I've inadvertently forgotten.

Abraham Lincoln: When the Moon Turned Away
Coconut: You're a Buttfaced Joni Mitchell
DC Poetry: A Unicorn Boner for Humanity
Eleven Eleven: Why Am I Suddenly Responsible for John Cougar Mellencamp's
  Castration Complex?; Why Am I Suddenly Loving Your Summery Goyish
  Om?; Why *Can't* I Be the Forlorn Mildew of Dorian Gray?
Evergreen Review: This Gorilla Called Philip Sidney
Hanging Loose: A Wedding Song
Mainstream Poetry: I Am Mormon Hot
Poetry: The Swiss Just Do Whatever
Poets for Living Waters: Pimp My Top-Feed Live-Kill Mothership
The Scream: I Am a Lonely Oneironaut, in Need of Salutary Grounding; I Am
  Now Bringing Everything to the Path; I Want to Expose Myself for Love of
  the People; I Am Cocked Up from Overpower
Truck: I Lost My Beatnik Antlers on the Grassy Knoll—Help Me, JFK; My
  Name in Hebrew; I Discovered Pain

West Wind Review: Why Am I So Angry with William Blake?; What Happens When Your Eyeball Falls out of the Socket?

WSQ/Women's Studies Quarterly: I Have Always Wanted an Emu

"I Am Cocked Up from Overpower" appeared, in a slightly different version, in the anthology *Viva la Difference: Poetry Inspired by the Paintings of Peter Saul*, published by Off the Park Press, 2010. (Thank you, Boni Joi.)

Sharon Mesmer is a poet, fiction writer, and essayist. Her previous poetry collections are *Annoying Diabetic Bitch* (Combo Books, 2008), *The Virgin Formica* (Hanging Loose Press, 2008), *Vertigo Seeks Affinities* (chapbook, Belladonna Books, 2007), *Half Angel, Half Lunch* (Hard Press, 1998) and *Crossing Second Avenue* (chapbook, ABJ Press, Tokyo, 1997). Her fiction collections are *Ma Vie à Yonago* (Hachette Littératures, Paris, in French translation by Daniel Bismuth, 2005), *In Ordinary Time* (Hanging Loose Press, 2005), and *The Empty Quarter* (Hanging Loose Press, 2005). She teaches in the undergraduate and graduate programs of New York University and the New School. Originally from Chicago, she has lived in Brooklyn, New York since 1988.

Praise for Sharon Mesmer

With great wit, the poetry of Sharon Mesmer plunders the new realism of digital space, with its wishes, lies, and "ever-shifting Brangelina alerts." Profane and delirious, this is the *Divine Comedy* of our postmodern Eden. —**Paul Hoover**

Whatever it is you need to take you beyond your humdrum life—emus, golden human women with kitten hands, clown deer, labial wings, the forlorn mildew of Dorian Gray, blintzes, pet fungal onions, toy anal ATMs, or tiny uni-cows—Sharon Mesmer's poetry has it. It's encyclopedic! It radiates comic intelligence with a rare ferocity, like a Borscht Belt act. Add to cart! —**Nada Gordon**

Parodying the come-ons of capitalism, Mesmer surprises us with access to something we hadn't considered wanting, an arch anger that is surprisingly accepting of the compromises situations push on people, while at the same time smoldering with acidic resentment, as if Mesmer forgave the compromiser only to feel doubly incensed at the leveraged situations prodding us to inauthenticity.
—**Stan Apps**, *Jacket*

No matter what form Mesmer's words are taking at the moment, jokes—actual jokes that go "hardy-har-har!" at you, me, "I," dogs, trees, astronauts—pop up like vermin in a Whack-a-mole game. No one is safe. Elbows, two-by-fours, knuckle sandwiches, and banana peels fly. Perhaps her most fixed form is that of Mesmie, the ninth Stooge. —**Jennifer L. Knox**, *Best American Poetry* **blog**

. . . always interesting, beautifully bold and vivaciously modern. —**Allen Ginsberg**

Sharon Mesmer's poetry is a stream of indomitable spunk . . . tough and lush . . . a fabulous tissue of language which floats out to inhabit other bodies, opens their mouths and makes them speak.
—**Alice Notley**

Sharon Mesmer, self-absorbed punk, writes outrageous language trying to be funny with bizarre juxtapositions, sometimes useful, sometimes as gratuitous as the language. I remember when I discovered Dada when I was in high school, and my friends and I sat around composing poems from random word searches in the dictionary (pre-Google) and laughing at our cleverness. Maybe I should dig out those old notebooks, and perhaps I too can get a good-paying gig in Academe.
—**Dan Wilcox**, *Albany Poets*

"I am indeed the John Hopkins who wrote "Expressed gene sequences of two variants of Sheep interleukin-25"

CPSIA information can be obtained
at www.ICGtesting.com
Printed in the USA
BVHW011006150522
637069BV00011B/229